RACHAEL RAY

By Jayne Keedle

People We Should Know

Gareth Stevens
Publishing

Please visit our web site at **www.garethstevens.com.**
For a free color catalog describing our list of high-quality books,
call 1-800-542-2595 (USA) or 1-800-387-3178 (Canada). Our fax: 1-877-542-2596

Library of Congress Cataloging-in-Publication Data
Keedle, Jayne.
   Rachael Ray / by Jayne Keedle.
      p. cm. — (People we should know)
   Includes bibliographical references and index.
    ISBN-10: 1-4339-2189-8   ISBN-13: 978-1-4339-2189-6 (lib. bdg.)
    ISBN-10: 1-4339-2149-9   ISBN-13: 978-1-4339-2149-0 (soft cover)
    1. Ray, Rachael—Juvenile literature. 2. Cooks—United States—Biography—Juvenile
 literature. I. Title.
   TX649.R29K44 2010
   641.5092—dc22   2009007169

This edition first published in 2010 by
Gareth Stevens Publishing
A Weekly Reader® Company
1 Reader's Digest Road
Pleasantville, NY 10570-7000 USA

Copyright © 2010 by Gareth Stevens, Inc.

Executive Managing Editor: Lisa M. Herrington
Senior Editor: Brian Fitzgerald
Senior Designer: Keith Plechaty

Produced by Editorial Directions, Inc.

Art Direction and Page Production: Kathleen Petelinsek, The Design Lab

Picture credits
Cover and title page: Jim Spellman/WireImage; p. 5, 40: Scott Gries/Getty Images; p. 6:
TWPhoto/Corbis; p. 8: Mark Von Holden/Getty Images; p. 9: Paul Drinkwater/NBCU Photo
Bank via AP Images; p. 11, 14, 15: Yearbook Library; p. 12: Rena Schild/Shutterstock; p.
16: iStock/demarco-media; p. 19: Mike Booth/Alamy; p. 20: Frank Paul/Alamy; p. 21: Gail
Oskin/WireImage; p. 22: AP Photo/Richard Drew; p. 25: Brad Barket/Getty Images; p. 26: Ali
Paige Goldstein/NBC NewsWire via AP Images; p. 28: Gilbert Carrasquillo/FilmMagic; p. 29:
Raymond Boyd/Michael Ochs Archives/Getty Images; p. 30: Mark Daniels for Every Day with
Rachel Ray Magazine/WireImage; p. 31: Diane Cohen/Everett Collection; p. 33, 43: King World
Prod./Courtesy: Everett Collection; p. 34: Todd Plitt/Getty Images; p. 36: Jean Baptiste Lacroix/
WireImage; p. 37: Phil McCarten/Reuters/Corbis; p. 39: Bryan Bedder/Getty Images; p. 41: AP
Photo/Lucas Jackson

Printed in the United States of America

1 2 3 4 5 6 7 8 9 14 13 12 11 10 09

TABLE OF CONTENTS

Words in the glossary appear in **bold** type
the first time they are used in the text.

CHAPTER 1

Creative Cooking

Rachael Ray had never been more nervous. On November 12, 2006, she was competing on *Iron Chef America*. The cooking competition on cable TV's Food Network gave top chefs one hour to cook four dishes. Each dish had to include an ingredient that was kept secret until the contest began.

Ray is an experienced cook, and she's used to being on TV. So why was she scared about cooking on *Iron Chef America*?

Rachael Ray tapes an episode of her TV show.

Facing Fear

Ray wasn't worried about having only an hour to cook. She is famous for making meals in 30 minutes! She wasn't nervous about cooking on camera. She was hosting four shows on the Food Network and had just launched *Rachael Ray*, her own talk show.

"I've always been afraid of this show because I'm not a chef," she explained. "I just cook." Facing off against "real chefs" worried Ray. "But that's why I wanted to do it," she said. "I wanted to face my fear."

Iron Chef

Iron Chef America is one of the Food Network's most popular shows. It's based on *Iron Chef*, a show in Japan. Both shows typically make two chefs go head-to-head in a timed cooking competition. Each of the four courses must contain the secret ingredient, which forces them to be creative. Past ingredients have included squid and asparagus. Ray's secret ingredient was cranberries.

A chef competes on the TV show *Iron Chef*.

Hot Under the Collar

It's rare for Ray to be afraid of anything, particularly in the kitchen. She grew up in the restaurant business and always felt safe behind a stove. On *Iron Chef*, she cooked with her friend chef Mario Batali against chefs Giada De Laurentiis and Bobby Flay.

The two teams raced around the kitchen. Judges rated the results on taste, creativity, and presentation. In spite of all her worries, Ray's team won! It was further proof that she could do anything she put her mind to.

Not Your Average Cook

Rachael Ray is different from other celebrity cooks. She didn't train to be a chef. She never wears a chef's hat or apron. Her food isn't fancy or hard to make. Ray wants to encourage her viewers to cook. Her specialty is "fast food." She shows people how to whip up yummy meals in the time it takes to have a pizza delivered. Her trademark is "30-Minute Meals." She says, "If I can do it, anybody can."

Ray makes cooking look like fun. She learned to cook from an early age and strongly believes in teaching kids to cook. "If kids are involved in making dinner and see that everyone else is taking pleasure in what they've done, they feel an enormous sense of pride," she told *Ladies' Home Journal*.

Fast Fact

In 2006, *Forbes* magazine named Rachael Ray the second most trusted celebrity. Actor Tom Hanks was first.

"I've encouraged people not to be afraid of cooking. ... Especially kids!"

–Rachael Ray

The School of Mama

Ray's family was in the restaurant business. Growing up, she did everything from washing dishes to waiting tables. Asked where she learned to cook, she is proud to say, "I went to the school of MAMA!" Her mother taught her much more than how to cook. "My mother raised us so that when an opportunity came up, we should take the risk," Ray explained.

Ray enjoys teaching kids how to cook.

Kids in the Kitchen

Ray's 2008 book, *Yum-O! The Family Cookbook*, includes 20 recipes chosen from thousands sent in by kids. Charnele Parker, 17, of Chicago, Illinois, was excited when her sandwich recipe was included in the book. She's a fan, she said, because Ray is relaxed even when she makes mistakes. "She made me laugh while she cooked," Charnele told the *Chicago Tribune*.

Ray appears on *The Tonight Show With Jay Leno* in 2006.

Food Fans

Today, Ray runs a food and **media** empire. She has written more than a dozen cookbooks, many of them best sellers. Her down-to-earth personality and relaxed approach to cooking have won her millions of fans. She never set out to be a chef and never dreamed she'd be famous. She just liked working with food. In 2006, *Time* magazine named Ray one of the top 100 most influential people in America. She earned that honor for "changing the way America cooks."

Fast Fact

Ray is now so famous that a wax figure of her is on display at Madame Tussauds wax museum in New York City.

CHAPTER 2

Kitchen Childhood

Rachael Domenica Ray was born on August 25, 1968, in Massachusetts. She grew up with an older sister, Maria, and a younger brother, Manny. Her mom, Elsa Scuderi, was the oldest of 10 children in a large Italian family. Her dad, James Ray, added a touch of **Cajun** spice to the family. He came from Louisiana.

Rachael Ray spent her early years living on Cape Cod, Massachusetts. Her parents ran three restaurants there.

Family Tradition

"I was in the kitchen watching my mother and learning about food even before I picked up a spoon!" Rachael wrote on her web site. "She'd have me on her hip while she stirred a pot on the stove and carried on a conversation."

Cooking and sharing meals together were key parts of Rachael's family life. Her first clear memory is watching her mom cook. "She was flipping something with a spatula. I tried to copy her and ended up grilling my right thumb!" Rachael recalled. "I was three or four."

Fast Fact

Rachael Ray's middle name is Domenica, which means "Sunday" in Italian.

Ray grew up in the town of Lake George. It is located on the shore of a beautiful lake.

Moving Upstate

In the early 1970s, Rachael's family moved to Lake George, a small town in the Adirondack Mountains in upstate New York. Her father got a job at a publishing company. Her mother worked as food supervisor for a chain of Howard Johnson restaurants. Rachael's mom worked long hours. Often, she took her kids to work with her. "She didn't want us with babysitters," Rachael said. "We all grew up in restaurants."

Getting Creative

As a child, Rachael suffered from **croup**. Croup is an infection that affects children under six. Rachael's vocal cords would swell, and she would cough a lot. To help her breathe, her parents used sheets and broomsticks to make a **vaporizing tent**. She would sit on her bed under the tent, writing and drawing for hours.

Rachael was a creative and active child. She would often get up in the middle of the night to draw or write. She wrote so much that she developed calluses (thickened areas of skin) on her fingers from holding a pencil!

Fast Fact

Rachael's mom recalled her daughter's first impression of school that "the food is bad and people can't read."

A Beloved Grandfather

Rachael's grandfather was a huge influence in her life. Emmanuel was an Italian immigrant. He moved from Gela, Sicily, to upstate New York, where he worked as a **stonemason**. His two passions were gardening and cooking for his family. With 10 children, there were many mouths to feed. "In my family, there was always good food. It was Italian stinky cheese, fresh greens, and sauces," Rachael recalled. "My grandfather and I were best friends."

Drawn Together

Rachael's parents divorced when she was 13. Her father moved to nearby Saratoga Springs, New York. The kids lived with their mom in Lake George. Still, the family remained close. "For a lot of people divorce is traumatic, but for us it made for a happier family," Rachael said. She knew that her parents would be better off living apart.

As the kids got older, they began helping their mom at work. Rachael was a hard worker. By high school, she had a part-time job as a waitress at the restaurants her mom managed. Early on, her family knew that she had ambition and a drive to succeed.

Rachael (far left) enjoyed singing in a youth choir.

Cheerleading was a favorite high school activity for Rachael (center).

Always Cheerful

Rachael wanted to climb to the top, and in high school she really did. She was a cheerleader for her school team, the Lake George Warriors. "I was the 'ta-dah!' cheerleader, the one who climbed to the top of the pyramid and then flipped into the arms of other cheerleaders," Ray said.

Rachael was still in high school when she started her own business. She made and delivered gift baskets. She'd often stay up late in her room, putting together baskets full of pasta and cocoa. She called her business Delicious **Liaisons**.

Fast Fact

Growing up, Rachael's favorite game was Boggle, which takes one minute to play!

College Daze

Rachael had always worked in restaurants. Still, she wasn't sure what she wanted to do for a living. After graduating from high school in 1986, she went to Pace University in New York. For the first time, Rachael was away from her family. She decided to study literature and communications. But after two years, she dropped out. College was expensive, and Rachael wasn't sure what she wanted to do with her life.

Bake Off!

When she was 15, Rachael tried to make a lemon cake for her mom. But she did something wrong, and the cake didn't rise. Rachael was so disappointed that she cried. She decided to leave the baking to her older sister, Maria, who is a whiz at it. Rachael's talents were in other areas. She had a knack for taking family recipes and finding ways to prepare them fast. Rachael calls it "canoodling" recipes.

A Casual Observer

When Rachael was a child, her favorite book was *The Casual Observer*. It was about a little girl who traveled the world, observing people and asking questions. One day, a teacher asked Rachael's classmates what they wanted to be when they grew up. When it was Rachael's turn, she answered, "A casual observer!"

Opportunity Knocks

Rachael returned to the Adirondacks and rented a cabin in the small town of Lake Luzerne. She found work at local restaurants. Still, she sometimes struggled to pay her rent. In the small town, there were few job opportunities.

Then Rachael saw a job listing in the *New York Times*. It was for someone to manage the candy counter at Macy's department store in New York City. "I could do that!" Rachael thought.

Fast Fact

Macy's main store in New York City opened in 1924 and was billed as the "world's largest store."

"She's always risen to the top."

–Maria Batar, talking about her younger sister, Rachael Ray

CHAPTER 3

The World of Food

Ray got the job at Macy's. She did so well at the candy counter that she was **promoted**. She became a buyer for Macy's fresh foods department. She learned about everything from buying cheese to putting together gift baskets for customers.

In 1993, Ray was offered a spot in Macy's management training program. But that would mean leaving the food department, so she said no. She now knew she wanted to work with food. Ray's time at Macy's helped her land her next job.

Ray's job at Macy's in New York City helped kick off her career.

A Scary Lesson

Ray became the manager of Agata & Valentina. The family-run **gourmet** market in New York City specializes in Sicilian food and wine. Ray felt at home at once. She loved her job. However, she didn't love life in New York City. When the same person tried to mug her twice in two weeks, she packed her bags and went home to her mom. "I felt the whole universe was telling me, 'You're not supposed to be here right now,' " Ray told *Vanity Fair*.

Ray worked at the Sagamore Hotel after leaving New York City.

A Cook Is Born

Ray got a job at the Sagamore Hotel, a famous resort in Lake George. Then she became a food buyer for a gourmet store in Albany, New York. She took on extra responsibility when the chef left. She began making the store's prepared meals.

Many people told Ray that they didn't know how to cook. Others said they didn't have time to cook. To boost grocery sales, Ray suggested the store offer cooking classes called "30 Minute **Mediterranean** Meals."

Fast Fact

Ray thought if people knew how to make a meal in half an hour, they would want to cook. That's how she came up with the idea for "30 Minute Meals."

Breaking News

The store's owners loved the idea. But Ray couldn't find a chef to teach the classes. When her boss asked Ray to teach them, she said she wasn't a chef. "Who cares?" the boss said. "Your food's good!"

Ray's cooking classes were a hit. Their popularity attracted the attention of the local TV news station. In 1999, the news show invited her to do a cooking segment. It turned into a weekly feature called "30 Minute Meals." At first, Ray didn't get paid for her appearances. But she hoped they might lead to other opportunities. Her optimism paid off.

Book It!

When local TV viewers began asking for Ray's recipes, she decided to put together a cookbook. She sent the manuscript to Hiroko Kiiffner, who ran a small publishing company called Lake Isle Press. Kiiffner published Ray's first book, called *30 Minute Meals*, in 1999. The book sold 10,000 copies at Price Chopper, a food warehouse store, in just two weeks, during the holidays. Three months later, it went into its second printing.

Ray's cooking was a big hit with the *Today* show's Al Roker.

A Big Break

In March 2001, **producers** for NBC's *Today* show were looking for someone to do a cooking segment. A snowstorm had forced many guests to cancel. One of the show's hosts, Al Roker, suggested the show contact Ray. He often watched her show at his house in upstate New York. Ray was shocked! This was her big break.

Ray was nervous about cooking on the *Today* show, but she handled it like a pro. Her friendly personality made her an instant hit with viewers. Someone from the Food Network saw the show that day. The next day, Ray got a call from Food Network executives. They wanted her to host her own show!

The Food Network

Just days after Ray appeared on the *Today* show, she met with Food Network producers. At that meeting, she said, "I clearly don't belong here, I'm not a chef." She got up to leave. And they said, "No, no, no, stop. That's what we like. We don't want you to be a chef."

The Food Network had plenty of programs hosted by famous chefs. Network executives were looking for someone who could reach a wider, younger audience.

The network offered Ray $360,000 to make 25 episodes of a show called *30 Minute Meals*. After years of struggling to make ends meet, Ray could hardly believe it. She used the money to buy the cabin she and her mom had been renting in Lake Luzerne.

66Rachael came along with the right idea at the right time.**99**

–Brooke Johnson, president of the Food Network

CHAPTER 4

Fast Food

"Hello, I'm Rachael Ray, and I make 30-minute meals!" That's how Ray introduced herself on her first show for the Food Network in 2001.

Ray stood out instantly from other chefs on the network. She didn't make complicated meals. She made foods most people were familiar with. She didn't measure ingredients. She'd direct viewers to add "half a palm-full" of an ingredient or "eyeball it" to see if that was enough. When she dropped something on the floor, she just giggled.

Ray's lively personality helps keep her cooking shows exciting.

A Human Cartoon

Ray had a blue-jeaned approach to cooking, and she wasn't about to dress it up. "I'm not wearing a chef coat," she told a reporter. "I'm as close to a human cartoon as you can get!"

Other celebrity chefs were horrified that Ray used ready-made ingredients, such as pre-chopped vegetables and cake mix. Some people said she shouldn't be teaching others how to cook. Ray was the first to agree. "I have no formal [training]," she cheerfully admitted. "I'm completely unqualified for any job I've ever had."

Fast Fact

Even though Ray grew up in New York, she is a Boston Red Sox fan.

The Anti-Martha Stewart

Ray's career path was similar to that of Martha Stewart (left), another TV show host famous for cooking and entertaining. Both seemed to become celebrities overnight. There was a big difference between the two, however. Martha Stewart is known as the perfect hostess everyone dreams of being. Ray is known as a klutz who drops things and spills ingredients. Also, she represents the average person who doesn't have a lot of time to cook. Perhaps that's why Ray became known as the anti-Martha Stewart.

Playing to the Home Crowd

"I'm not a chef, I'm a cook," Ray said in an interview with *Esquire* magazine. "But even the best chef in the world needs to know how to make a fast, tasty burger."

Ray's fans loved her! Her relaxed attitude toward cooking was **contagious**. If Ray said a dish was "awesome" and "easy peasy," people believed her. What's more, they were encouraged to try making it themselves at home. "She empowers the home cook," said celebrity chef Bobby Flay.

Becoming a Star

30 Minute Meals owed much of its success to its host. Ray was a star, but she also seemed like the girl next door. Soon the Food Network asked Ray to host a second show. Called *$40 a Day*, it was launched in 2002. Ray's job was to find places where people could dine out for just $40 each day. From her early years of having trouble paying the rent, she knew how to stretch a buck!

Hitting the Road

Filming *$40 a Day* took Ray out of the kitchen and on the road. She went in search of the best ice cream stands, hot dog stands, and picnic spots. She proved to viewers that even if they were traveling, they could eat good food and stick to a budget.

Taping *30 Minute Meals* and *$40 a Day* kept Ray busy. Still, she found time to write another cookbook in 2001. It was called *Comfort Foods: Rachael Ray's 30-Minute Meals*. She also found time for romance.

Fast Fact

While filming the first episode of *30 Minute Meals*, Ray cut her finger. She used Krazy Glue to close the wound so she could finish filming!

John Cusimano joins Rachael Ray at a taping in New York City's Bryant Park.

Perfect Partners

In 2002, Ray met John Cusimano, a lawyer and rock musician, at a party. Their friends say it was love at first sight. "I was speechless, and I'm never speechless!" Ray told *People* magazine.

In 2003, Cusimano joined Ray on a book tour for *30-Minute Meals 2*. He noticed that a lot of people asked Ray what kind of knives and cookware she used. The time seemed right for Ray to launch her own line of kitchenware. Soon Ray had her own brand of knives, cookware, and food processors.

Fast Fact

When they were dating, Cusimano wrote a song for Ray called "Burn." It was about burning love, though, not burning food!

Booking Along

When Ray wasn't taping her programs for the Food Network, she was writing. In 2004, she published four cookbooks. *Cooking Rocks! Rachael Ray 30-Minute Meals for Kids* was the first of several cookbooks Ray would write to encourage kids to cook. Another was a spin-off from her show *$40 a Day*.

"All the books are based largely on *30 Minute Meals*," Ray told the *Miami Herald*. "I try to keep it fresh, and I also try to keep it cheap and cheerful." She always made sure her books cost no more than a DVD or music CD.

Best-Selling Author

Many of Ray's books became best sellers. That's unusual for cookbooks. In fact, her friend Mario Batali credits her with changing the cookbook market. "Someone sells 50,000 copies of a book, it used to be considered very nice," Batali explained. "She's created a market where she can do two or three books in a year and they'll all sell a million copies."

Wedding Bells

On September 24, 2005, Rachael Ray and John Cusimano got married at a castle in Tuscany, Italy. Ray paid for her 100 guests to fly to the wedding. With a successful career and a new husband, she didn't need anything else to make her happy. So instead of asking for gifts, the couple asked friends to make donations to animal rescue charities.

Rachael Ray and John Cusimano celebrate their wedding day.

Star Power

By 2004, *30 Minute Meals* had become one of the Food Network's top-rated shows. Although Ray was becoming a celebrity, she didn't act like a star. Fans greeted her with a "Hey, Rach!" and a hug, as if they'd known her for years.

Her next show, *Inside Dish*, was launched in 2004. It took Ray into the kitchens of celebrities. She'd hang out with Raven-Symoné, for instance, who would show her how she made baked ziti. Ray was excited to meet big stars.

Fast Fact

Ray's book *365: No Repeats* offers a different recipe for every day of the year.

Food Around the World

In 2005, the Food Network signed up Ray for a fourth show. The *Tasty Travels* show had Ray eating her way around the world. She visited European cities and other exotic places. She often took her mom and husband along for the trip.

Cover Girl

By 2005, Ray had nearly 4.5 million books in print and was working on her 11th title. Meanwhile, Ray branched out to the magazine business. In October, she launched *Every Day with Rachael Ray*. The lifestyle magazine featured articles about food and family, with recipes and tips. It was the most successful magazine launch of the year.

Fast Fact

The debut of *Tasty Travels* attracted the second-largest audience the Food Network had ever had for a new show.

In 2005, Ray's magazine hit the newsstands.

CHAPTER 5

Recipe for Success

Rachael Ray is very chatty and loves to meet new people. So she was quite at home as a guest on talk shows. Her many appearances on the *Oprah Winfrey Show* led to something new.

Winfrey is one of the most powerful women in the entertainment industry. She suggested that Ray should host her own talk show. Ray wasn't sure if she'd be as successful in a show that wasn't about food. But Winfrey encouraged her. "You have got it!" Winfrey told her. "Just be you!"

It didn't take long for Rachael Ray and Oprah Winfrey to become good friends.

Another TV Show

Ray thought it was worth a try. However, she didn't want her name to be in the show's title. "It's way too much about me!" Ray said. The producer, Terry Wood, managed to change Ray's mind about that. The show would be called *Rachael Ray*.

There was one thing that Ray was firm about, however. "There will be no crying on my show!" she said. Ray wanted her show to be as upbeat as she was. The show would include some cooking, some celebrity interviews, and solutions to everyday problems.

Fast Fact

People magazine named *Rachael Ray* one of the top 10 shows of 2006.

Television Talk

The first *Rachael Ray* show aired on September 18, 2006. It was broadcast nationally and attracted high ratings for a talk show **premiere**. Ray has always said she feels safest behind a stove. With that in mind, the set of her show included a kitchen and cooking demonstrations. Ray's guests would join her to chat around the kitchen table. Often they'd help her cook, too.

Ray's friendly face and girl-next-door appeal attracted viewers of all ages. This came as no surprise to Wood. Her own seven-year-old daughter was a fan of Ray's. Wood's daughter told her that she just liked Ray's face. *Time* magazine raved that Ray was "gifted at being on television."

Ray tapes one of the first episodes of her talk show, *Rachael Ray*.

What's the Word?

Ray often makes up words to describe her food. She calls sandwiches "sammies." She uses "stoup" to describe soups that are as thick as stews. She calls mozzarella cheese "motz" and shortens extra-virgin olive oil to "EVOO." Her meals may be delicious and nutritious, but Ray says they are "delish" and "nutrish." Her favorite made-up word is Yum-O. "It's a combination of 'Yummy!' and 'Oh wow!' " Ray explains.

A People Person

Rachael Ray was the first show Ray had done in front of a live audience. On *30 Minute Meals*, she joked, she'd been talking to vegetables for years! She wasn't nervous on live TV, though. "I feed off the energy of the audience, even when I'm taping three shows in one day," she told the *Seattle Post-Intelligencer*.

Ray likes to talk to her fans. Signing books in stores, she says, gives her a chance to get feedback from readers. "They are my boss at the end of the day," Ray says of her readers. "I'm still a waitress, and I want to bring my customers what they want."

Fast Fact

In 2006, EVOO was included in the *Oxford American College Dictionary* as the abbreviation for "extra-virgin olive oil."

Yum-O!

In 2006, Ray put her money where her mouth is. She founded a charity called Yum-O! With its partner organizations, Yum-O! aims to address the problem of hunger and poor nutrition in the United States. In 2007, an estimated 12.4 million children didn't eat nutritious meals regularly. Unhealthy eating habits can lead to people being overweight and suffering from illnesses such as diabetes and heart disease.

Ray started the charity to help families learn how to cook nutritious meals. She also hopes to inspire kids to learn to cook. "We want to help parents and kids enjoy cooking together," she says.

Ray helps a young cook prepare a healthy meal.

Living Her Dream

In 2008, *Rachael Ray* won a Daytime **Emmy Award** for outstanding talk show. The show was doing so well in the ratings that *Rachael Ray* was renewed until 2010.

Also that year, Ray devoted one episode of her talk show to a "Wedding Rescue." She arranged and paid for 40 couples to get married after a hurricane in Texas forced them to cancel their weddings. Country music star Wynonna Judd played at the reception. It was the only show where Ray allowed crying. "Get your Kleenex ready," Ray said in an interview with the *Miami Herald*. "[They] were the most beautiful brides I have ever seen."

Fast Fact

In 2007, Ray appeared on an episode of *Sesame Street*. She introduced "pumpernickel" as the word of the day.

CHAPTER 6

What's Cooking?

Ray has worked hard to achieve her success. She puts in long hours and sleeps no more than five hours a night. Her father describes her as "the hardest working person I know."

Always on the move, in 2008, Ray launched another show on the Food Network. Called *Rachael's Vacation*, it was a travel show that paid her to take vacations. Ray loves cooking, traveling, writing, and meeting people. Her career was paying her about $16 million a year to do just that!

Actor John Stamos (left) joins Ray on her TV show.

Branching Out

Ray is grateful for everything she has. She is happy to share some of her wealth through Yum-O! In 2008, she also started Rachael's Rescue to help animals that have been neglected or abused. She launched a line of pet food, Rachael Ray Nutrish for pets. A portion of the proceeds goes to help animals in need.

Puppy Love

Ray loves animals, particularly her dog, Isaboo. When her first pit bull, Boo, died suddenly in 2004, Ray was heartbroken. "I miss my girl Boo every minute of every day," Ray wrote on her web site. Ray and her husband searched online to find another dog. They fell in love with a pit bull pup that looked a lot like their beloved Boo. They named the pup Isaboo.

Ray poses with Isaboo at an animal charity event.

Media Queen

By 2009, Ray had five shows on the Food Network. Her first show, *30 Minute Meals*, was still drawing more than a million U.S. viewers on weekends. She had brought home an Emmy for her highly rated *Rachael Ray* show.

Ray had also become the spokesperson for Dunkin' Donuts, Price Chopper food warehouse, and Nabisco Wheat Thins and Triscuits. The affordable products seemed a good fit for her. Ray's own line of products, meanwhile, had expanded to include bed and bath wares.

Fast Fact

One of Ray's kitchen products is called a Moppine, a combination of a dish towel and an oven mitt.

There's No Place Like Home

Rachael Ray is famous. However, being surrounded by friends and family in her hometown keeps her grounded. "Nobody treats me like a celebrity in my hometown," Ray told her local newspaper. "I love to travel, but like Dorothy said [in *The Wizard of Oz*], there's no place like home."

Ray's cabin on Lake Luzerne is just 12 miles (19 kilometers) from where she went to high school. It's far from luxurious. There's dirt under the wooden floors and not even a dishwasher in the kitchen. Yet Ray is happiest there, testing out new recipes in the kitchen on her mom, her husband, and Isaboo.

Rachael Ray and producer Terry Wood talk about the *Rachael Ray* show.

Throat Clearing

In December 2008, the throat problems of Ray's youth came back to haunt her. This time, she had a different diagnosis. Doctors thought she might need surgery to remove a polyp, a small lump that had developed in her throat. Instead of surgery, however, Ray was able to treat the problem with throat therapy. This was a better choice for Ray. If she had had surgery, she wouldn't have been able to talk for six weeks!

A Wonderful Accident

Rachael Ray's creators aim for her show to run at least until 2019. Terry Wood, the show's producer, said, "I think she could be on television as long as she wants to."

Ray never expected to be in this position. "My life has been a total accident," she wrote on her web site, "a very happy, wonderful accident that I didn't [plan] and couldn't have planned." Yet, every experience in Ray's life had prepared her for success.

> **"I got a job that's so great that I can't believe it's a job!"**
>
> –Rachael Ray, on why she loves her work

Hard work and a love for food have helped Ray to achieve her goals.

Happy Endings

Happily married, wealthy, and famous for doing the things she loves best, Ray is on top of the world. Yet in her mind, she continues to see herself as a waitress from a small town in New York.

"People ask me a lot, 'If you weren't doing this what would you be doing?'" Ray says. "I'd still be working in food. I was a happy waitress, a happy bartender, a happy cook, a happy everything, except dishwasher!" Rachael Ray believes that food "is about sharing; it's about expressing yourself; it's about bringing together different generations."

Fast Fact

Ray goes back to her high school in Lake George every year to speak to students. She encourages them to consider careers in food.

Time Line

1968 — Rachael Domenica Ray is born on August 25 in Massachusetts.

1993 — Ray leaves her job at Macy's to become a food buyer for a gourmet Italian market in New York City.

2001 — Ray makes her first national television appearance on the *Today* show.

2002 — Ray hosts *$40 a Day* on the Food Network. She meets John Cusimano, the man she will marry.

2003 — Ray publishes the cookbook *30-Minute Meals 2* and launches her own line of kitchen products.

2005 — Ray launches *Every Day with Rachael Ray* magazine. She and John Cusimano marry.

2006 — Ray founds Yum-O! She wins *Iron Chef America* and launches her daytime talk show, *Rachael Ray.*

2007 — Ray becomes a spokesperson for several companies. She expands her line of household products.

2008 — Ray wins an Emmy for best talk show. She publishes two cookbooks, bringing her total to 20.

Glossary

Cajun: people of French descent who moved from Acadia, Canada, to settle in Louisiana. Cajun cooking is known for its spiciness.

contagious: easily spread to others

croup: a disease that causes coughing and difficulty in breathing

Emmy Award: an award given to people who work in the television industry

gourmet: describing food that is high quality and often expensive

liaisons: close connections or relationships. The word *liaison* originally described a cooking ingredient that was used to bond and thicken sauces.

media: outlets such as television, magazines, newspapers, and the Internet that provide information to large numbers of people

Mediterranean: having to do with the food and culture of countries bordering the Mediterranean Sea. These countries include Greece, Morocco, Spain, Italy, Cyprus, and many others.

premiere: the first showing of a TV program or film

producers: people who are in charge of making a TV program, movie, play, or CD

promoted: moved to a more important job

stonemason: a person who is skilled at preparing stone for building

vaporizing tent: a tent that holds in moisture and heat

Find Out More

Books

Rau, Dana Meachen. *Chefs* (Tools We Use). Tarrytown, NY: Benchmark Books, 2008.

Ray, Rachael. *Cooking Rocks! Rachael Ray 30-Minute Meals for Kids*. New York: Lake Isle Press, 2004.

Ray, Rachael. *Yum-O! The Family Cookbook*. New York: Clarkson Potter, 2008.

Thompson, Lisa. *Creating Cuisine: Have You Got What It Takes to Be a Chef?* (On the Job). Minneapolis: Compass Point Books, 2008.

Web Sites

Every Day with Rachael Ray magazine
www.rachaelraymag.com
Find out the latest from Ray's magazine.

The Food Network: Rachael Ray
www.foodnetwork.com/rachael-ray/index.html
Watch a clip from Ray's show and follow a link to her bio.

Rachael Ray
www.rachaelray.com
Rachael Ray's official web site offers the latest news about her show, her cooking, and what's going on in her life.

Yum-O!
www.yum-o.org
Learn more about Ray's charity organization.

Source Notes

p. 5: *Iron Chef America*, Food Network, November 12, 2006; available online at www.youtube.com/watch?v=IEKdQamNe8U.

p. 7: Roberta Caploe, "Rachael Ray: A Ray of Sunshine," *Ladies' Home Journal,* August 2008, www.lhj.com/style/covers/rachael-ray-a-ray-of-sunshine/.

pp. 7, 11, 36, 43: "A Message from Rachael Ray," Yum-O! http://yum-o.org/message.php.

p. 8: Bill Daley, "Rachael Ray's book honors Chicago girl's recipe," *Chicago Tribune*, May 5, 2008, http://leisureblogs.chicagotribune.com/thestew/2008/05/rachel-rays-boo.html.

pp. 8, 12, 13: Stacey Morris, "Rachael Ray: School of Mama," *The Albany Times Union,* May 10, 2006, www.staceymorris.com/articles/RachaelRay.html.

p. 9: Mario Batali, "Rachael Ray," *Time*, April 30, 2006, www.time.com/time/magazine/article/0,9171,1187293,00.html.

p. 11, 42: Rachael Ray biography at www.rachaelrayshow.com/show-info/rachaels-bio/

p. 14: "Rachael Ray: Blurbs," TV.com, www.tv.com/rachael-ray/person/233190/trivia.html.

p. 14: Internet Movie Database, Rachael Ray Biography, www.imdb.com/name/nm1301904/bio

pp. 15, 26, 35, 42: John Marshall, "Rachael Ray's energy and success keep her going and going," *Seattle Post-Intelligencer*, December 18, 2006.

pp. 17, 19, 21, 23, 29, 38: Laura Jacobs, "Just Say Yum-O!" *Vanity Fair*, September 11, 2007, www.vanityfair.com/fame/features/2007/10/rachaelray200710.

pp. 17, 41: "Rachael Ray—Food Network's Waitress-Turned-Foodie Answers Our Questions." Budget Travel, August 1, 2005

p. 24: Rachael Ray, *30 Minute Meals*, season 1, episode 1, The Food Network

p. 25: Kim Severson, "Being Rachael Ray: How Cool Is That?" *New York Times*, October 19, 2005, www.nytimes.com/2005/10/19/dining/19rach.html.

pp. 25, 41: Paul Post, "Yum-O! Food Network star comes back to visit hometown," *The Saratogian*, April 25, 2007, www.saratogian.com/articles/2007/04/25/todays%20stories/18262422.txt.

p. 26: Rachael Ray, "The Indefensible Position: Rachael Ray Doesn't Suck," *Esquire* magazine, October 2006

pp. 26, 32, 33, 42: "Rachael Ray," *E! True Hollywood Story*, first aired on E! Entertainment Network, May 5, 2007.

p. 28: "Rachael Ray's Cookin' Career," *People*, September 16, 2006, www.people.com/people/article/0,,1535364,00.html.

pp. 29, 35, 37, 43: "Rachael Ray Keeps Cookin'," *Miami Herald*, November 20, 2008.

p. 33: Paul Maniaci, "Rachael Ray," *The Career Cookbook*, September 3, 2006, www.thecareercookbook.com/article.php?article_id=25.

p. 40: Rachael Ray, "Puppy Love," Every Day With Rachael Ray, February-March 2006, http://www.rachaelraymag.com/recipes/pet-food-recipes/pet-friendly---puppy-love/article.html

Index

About the Author

Jayne Keedle is a longtime journalist and former editor for *Weekly Reader*. As a freelance writer and editor, she is the author of a number of books for young adults. She shares her home in Connecticut with her husband, Jim; her stepdaughter, Alma; Snuffles the chocolate Lab; and Phoenix the cat. Jayne's husband is the cook in the family!